CW01249311

Like a Pro
Gymnastics

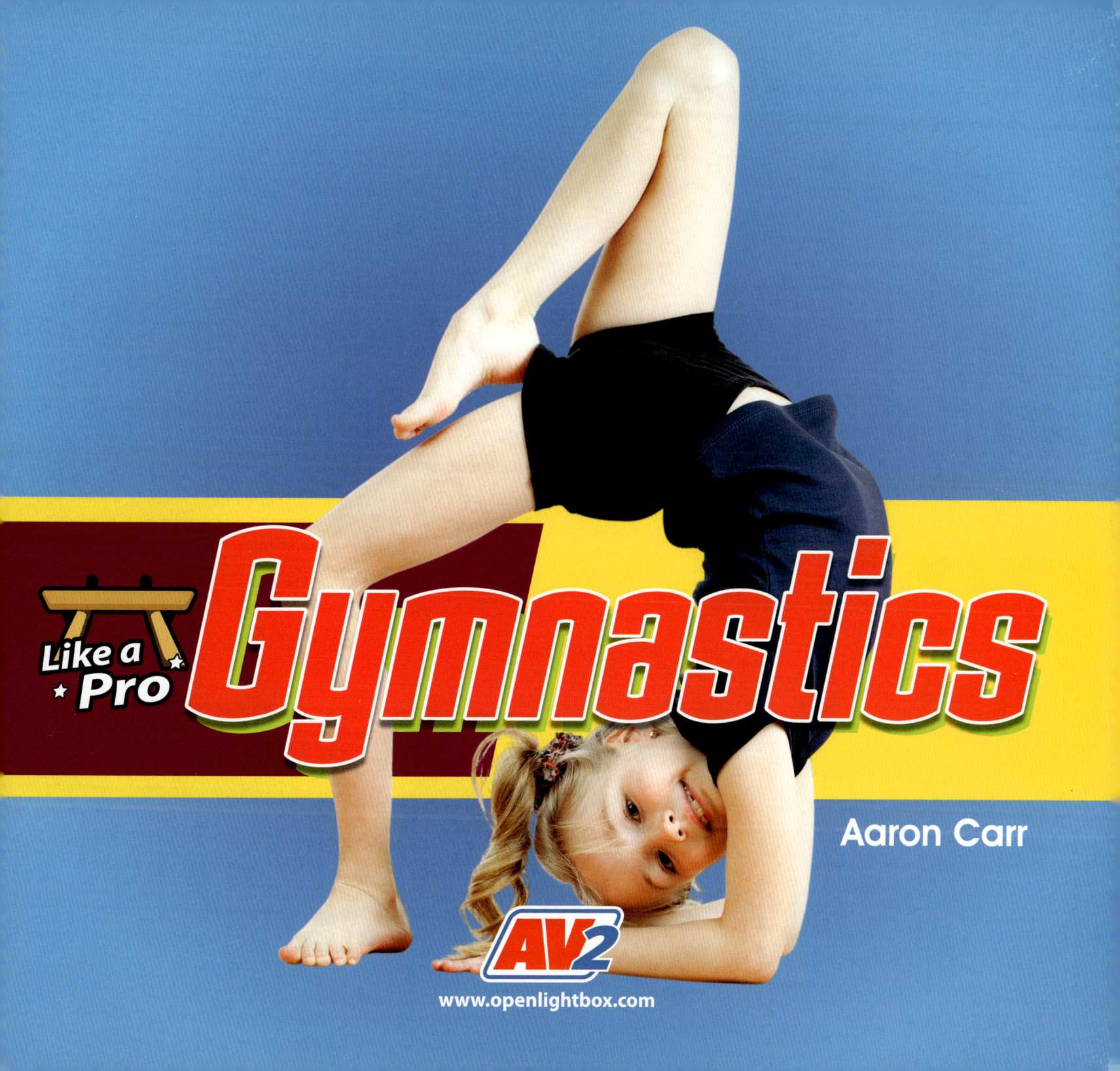

Aaron Carr

AV2

www.openlightbox.com

AV2

Step 1
Go to www.openlightbox.com

Step 2
Enter this unique code
FMYHWXO8W

Step 3
Explore your interactive eBook!

Your interactive eBook comes with...

Gymnastics

Start!

AV2 is optimized for use on any device

Read

Audio
Listen to the entire book read aloud

Videos
Watch informative video clips

Weblinks
Gain additional information for research

Try This!
Complete activities and hands-on experiments

Key Words
Study vocabulary, and complete a matching word activity

Quizzes
Test your knowledge

Slideshows
View images and captions

Share
Share titles within your Learning Management System (LMS) or Library Circulation System

Citation
Create bibliographical references following the Chicago Manual of Style

This title is part of our AV2 digital subscription

1-Year K–5 Subscription
ISBN 978-1-7911-3320-7

Access hundreds of AV2 titles with our digital subscription.
Sign up for a FREE trial at **www.openlightbox/trial**

Like a Pro
Gymnastics

Contents

- 2   AV2 Book Code
- 4   Getting Ready
- 6   What I Wear
- 8   What I Need
- 10 Where I Play
- 12 Warming Up
- 14 Artistic Gymnastics
- 16 Rhythmic Gymnastics
- 18 Part of the Team
- 20 I Love Gymnastics
- 22 Gymnastics Facts
- 24 Key Words

I love gymnastics.
I am going to do
gymnastics today.

Like a Pro

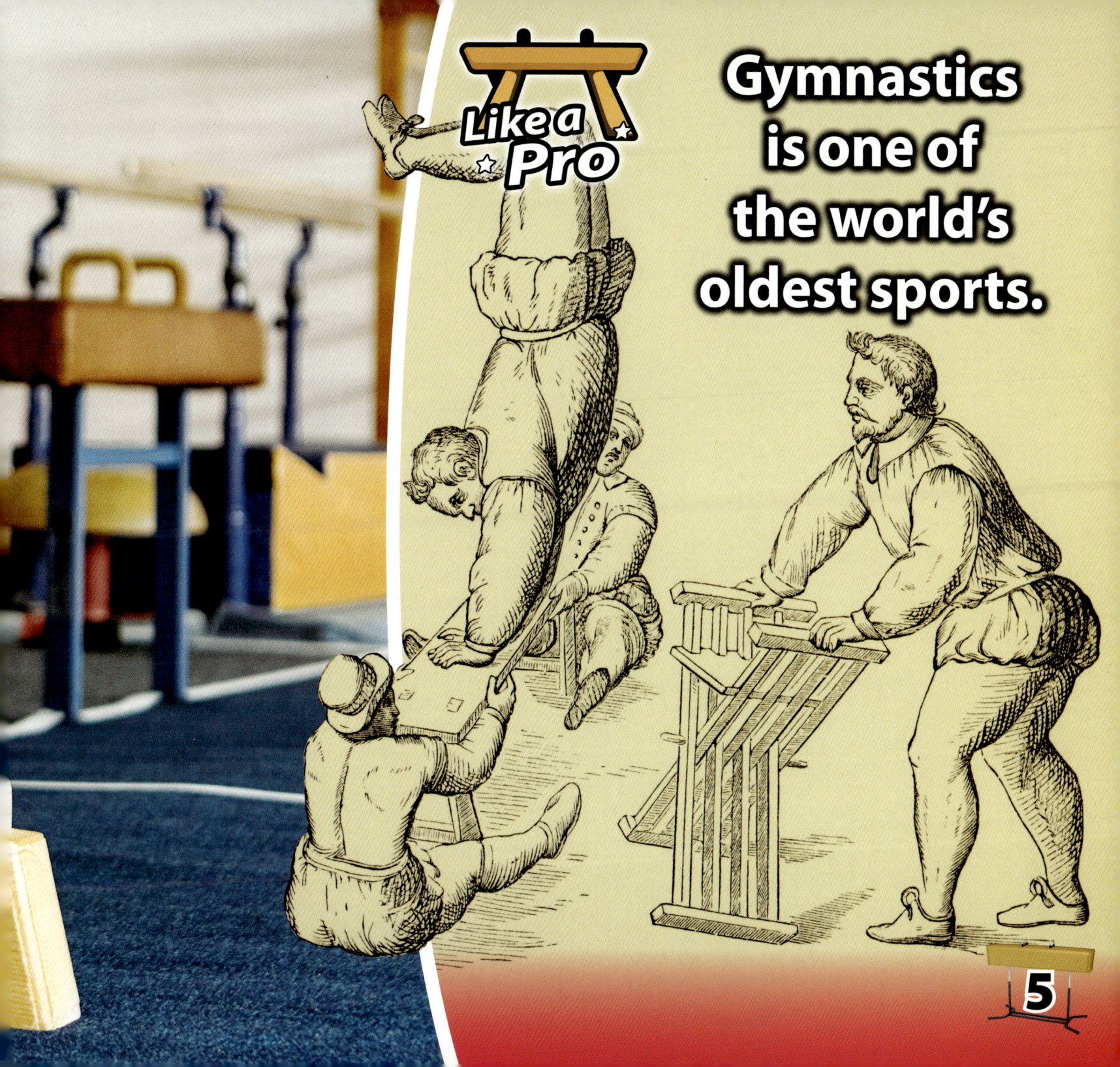

Gymnastics is one of the world's oldest sports.

I put on special clothes for gymnastics. I wear a one-piece leotard.

Like a Pro

Boys wear stirrup pants or shorts.

7

I use chalk to keep my hands dry. Chalking my hands keeps me from slipping.

Like a Pro

Some gymnasts wear grips on their hands.

9

I go to a gym for gymnastics classes. The gym has an area for each gymnastics event.

Like a Pro

Gyms often have a foam pit to help gymnasts practice safely.

11

I start by stretching and warming up my muscles. This helps me get ready to do gymnastics.

Like a Pro

Gymnasts must be very flexible.

13

I do artistic gymnastics.
My best event is the balance beam.

14

Like a Pro

There are four events for girls and six for boys.

15

My sister does rhythmic gymnastics. She does jumps and tricks with a hoop.

Like a Pro

Only girls do competitive rhythmic gymnastics.

17

I am part of a gymnastics team. Each person on the team does many different events.

Like a Pro

Teams can win gold, silver, and bronze medals.

19

20

I love gymnastics.

21

GYMNASTICS FACTS

These pages provide more detail about the interesting facts found in the book. They are intended to be used by adults as a learning support to help young readers round out their knowledge of each sport featured in the *Like a Pro* series.

Pages 4–5

Getting Ready The modern sport of gymnastics originated in ancient Greece. In fact, the word *gymnastics* comes from the Greek word for "exercise." Exercises that became popular in early Greek gymnasiums later became the gymnastic events at the first Olympic Games. These sports changed over the next 2,000 years. Today, the only gymnastic events that resemble the originals are tumbling and vaulting.

Pages 6–7

What I Wear Gymnasts wear tight-fitting clothing for a full range of motion. Girls usually wear a leotard. It may be sleeveless or have full-length sleeves. Boys wear a leotard and stirrup pants for most events. These tight-fitting pants have tapered legs and a strap that hooks under each foot. Boys wear shorts in vault and floor events. Most gymnasts do not wear anything on their feet. However, some wear special gymnastics shoes or toe caps.

Pages 8–9

What I Need Gymnasts chalk their hands, legs, and feet. This absorbs sweat and keeps the skin dry. Chalk helps gymnasts keep a strong grip. Without it, swinging from bars, hanging from rings, and balancing on high beams would be even more challenging and dangerous. The chalk used in gymnastics is usually a powder, although it can also be a solid block or a liquid. Liquid chalk turns to powder when applied to skin.

Pages 10–11

Where I Play People go to gymnasiums to do gymnastics. These gyms may be designed for gymnastics, or they may be traditional gyms with gymnastics equipment. A gymnastics gym usually has separate areas for each apparatus. Many gyms also have a large hole in the floor that is filled with foam blocks. This allows gymnasts to practice without fear of injury. Most gymnastics clubs offer classes for boys and girls of all ages, with separate classes for recreational and competitive training.

Pages 12–13

Warming Up A good warm-up routine helps to increase flexibility and decrease the risk of injury. This routine should start slow and easy, gradually getting more intense. Gymnasts may start with a walk or jog, then move on to stretches that target all of the main muscle groups. Stretches should start with something simple, such as arm circles, and build up to more advanced stretches, including the splits. Stretching helps loosen and lengthen muscles, which improves range of motion.

Pages 14–15

Artistic Gymnastics What most people think of as gymnastics is actually one form of the sport called artistic gymnastics. In artistic gymnastics, girls compete in balance beam, uneven bars, vault, and floor routine. Boys compete in parallel bars, horizontal bar, rings, pommel horse, vault, and floor exercise. In each event, gymnasts perform complex routines made up of many moves that require skill, strength, and flexibility. They earn a score for their routine based on its difficulty and the style and precision with which they perform the moves.

Pages 16–17

Rhythmic Gymnastics Rhythmic gymnastics is one of the other main forms of the sport. This type of gymnastics mixes elements of gymnastic exercises, ballet, and apparatus work. Rhythmic gymnasts perform four different routines on a 42.7- by 42.7-foot (13- by 13-meter) mat. Each routine features music and the use of a different piece of equipment, such as a ball, a hoop, a ribbon, a rope, or clubs. Gymnasts earn points for the artistic merits and difficulty of their routines. Execution is also part of their score, with points deducted for any mistakes a gymnast makes.

Pages 18–19

Part of the Team In addition to individual events, gymnasts also compete as a team. There are usually six members on a team, though this may change from one competition to another. Usually, only a set number of gymnasts compete in each event. In the Olympic artistic gymnastics finals, a team assigns three members to compete in each event. Some members may compete in one or two events, while others may compete in all events. Each member's score is added to determine the team score. The team with the highest score wins.

Pages 20–21

I Love Gymnastics Gymnastics is a high-energy and physically demanding sport. Taking part in gymnastics improves strength, speed, agility, flexibility, and physical awareness. It also promotes physical fitness and cardiovascular health. In order to have the strength and energy needed for gymnastics, it is important to eat a balanced diet. Fruits, vegetables, grains, and protein give the body the energy it needs to perform its best.

KEY WORDS

Research has shown that as much as 65 percent of all written material published in English is made up of 300 words. These 300 words cannot be taught using pictures or learned by sounding them out. They must be recognized by sight. This book contains 52 common sight words to help young readers improve their reading fluency and comprehension. This book also teaches young readers several important content words, such as proper nouns. These words are paired with pictures to aid in learning and improve understanding.

Page	Sight Words First Appearance
4	am, do, I, to
5	a, is, like, of, one, the, world
6	for, on, put
7	boys, or
8	from, hands, keep, me, my, use
9	some, their
10	an, each, go, has
11	have, help, often
12	and, by, get, start, this, up
13	be, must, very
15	are, four, girls, there
16	does, she, with
17	only
18	different, many, part
19	can

Page	Content Words First Appearance
4	gymnastics
5	pro, sports
6	clothes, leotard
7	shorts, stirrup pants
8	chalk
9	grips, gymnasts
10	area, classes, event, gym
11	foam pit
12	muscles
14	artistic gymnastics, balance beam
16	hoop, jumps, rhythmic gymnastics, sister, tricks
18	person, team
19	medals

Published by Lightbox Learning Inc.
276 5th Avenue, Suite 704 #917
New York, NY 10001
Website: www.openlightbox.com

Copyright ©2023 Lightbox Learning Inc.
All rights reserved. No part of this publication may be reproduced, stored in a retrieval system, or transmitted in any form or by any means, electronic, mechanical, photocopying, recording, or otherwise, without the prior written permission of the publisher.

Library of Congress Control Number: 2022934154

ISBN 978-1-7911-4848-5 (hardcover)
ISBN 978-1-7911-4849-2 (softcover)
ISBN 978-1-7911-4850-8 (multi-user eBook)

042022
100921

Printed in Guangzhou, China
1 2 3 4 5 6 7 8 9 0 26 25 24 23 22

Project Coordinator: John Willis
Designer: Jean Faye Marie Rodriguez

Every reasonable effort has been made to trace ownership and to obtain permission to reprint copyright material. The publisher would be pleased to have any errors or omissions brought to its attention so that they may be corrected in subsequent printings.

The publisher acknowledges Alamy, Dreamstime, Getty Images, and Shutterstock as its primary image suppliers for this title.